Earn Extra Money with a Sandwich Delivery Business

Jane Thomas

Copyright © 2013 by Jane Thomas

Published by - Samoht Publishing
samohtpublishing@mail.com

All rights reserved.
No part of this book may be reproduced by any mechanical, photographic, or electronic process, or in the form of a phonographic recording, nor may it be stored in a retrieval system, transmitted, or otherwise be copied for public or private use – other than for "fair use" as brief quotations embedded in articles and reviews without prior written permission of the publisher Samoht Publishing.

The intent of the author is only to offer information of a general nature to help you in your quest for knowledge. In the event you use any of the information in this book for yourself, which is your constitutional right, the author or publisher takes no responsibility in your actions.

ISBN-13: 978-1490402802
ISBN-10: 1490402802

Photo Acknowledgements
Cover photo by
Mathew Valencia from flickr.com
Inside photo by
dreamtime.com

DEDICATION

This book is dedicated to all those people who wish to take control of their own destiny and to profit from their hard work and dedication.

To all of you who read this book in the hope of bettering yourselves I wish you all the best luck in the world.

CONTENTS

Introduction 9
Part One – Getting Started 13
Research Your Area 15
Licenses and Permits 18
Calculating Your Profit Margin 22
Items You Will Need 27
The Next Step 30
Once Your are Up and Running 32
Part Two – Operating your Business 35
Getting Yourself Organised 37
Door to Door Business 40
Made to Order Business 45
Keeping the Books 49
Recipes 51
Meat Sandwiches 53
Vegetarian Sandwiches 58
Soups 61
Cakes 64
Metric Conversions 67
In Conclusion 69
History of the Humble Sandwich 70
Other Books by this Publisher 72

ACKNOWLEDGEMENTS

I would like to thank my husband for being so supportive while I concentrated on writing this book and for becoming my guinea pig on all my new sandwich recipes.

The book is a reflection of what you can do if you put your mind to it.

I've enjoyed creating my own business and have met many interesting people on the way. They know who they are.

Lastly to my daughter Claire for being my cake taster and bowl licker-outer, thank you my lovely girl, you have always been the best critic anyone could want.

INTRODUCTION

Ever thought how nice it would be to have some more money? Or maybe even a full-time income from only part-time hours? Well, you are not alone. Whenever money seems to get a bit tight we all try looking at different ways to find that elusive extra income.

Let's face it, there are many get rich quick schemes out there, but in all honesty the majority just don't work. They all seem geared up so that they are the ones who get rich, while you just end up a little poorer.

But there is a way of making an extra income on a regular basis that is also easy to get up and running quickly and without too much fuss either.

Delivering sandwiches might not be something you had ever considered before, but reading this book might just make you think again.

Take it from someone who has done it - and knows how it works - it really can give you that much needed extra income you have been dreaming of.

And don't forget, this is mostly a cash business so there is no need to wait months before you see any of the profits.

What you will learn from reading this book is expert information on how to start, and build up your sandwich delivery business with tried and tested methods along with recipes for sandwiches, soups and also cakes.

I teach you the best ways to promote your business - how to target specific outlets, as well as how to control the running costs.

You will also learn the best way to prepare the sandwiches, what fillings work best, and how to present your business in a smart and customer friendly manner.

And for those customers with special dietary needs we will also look at some healthy options and vegetarian alternatives.

We will also cover how to keep up to date records for both accounts and customers preferences.

In this day and age when so many people seem chained to their desks, a sandwich delivery business can be a god-send, especially for those who don't have the time or are sick and tired of making their own soggy and mundane sandwiches.

And this is where you come in! This is a sure fired

winner with all busy people. No matter what part of the world you look to operate this business in, it will work anywhere. We all need to eat and you will be filling that need.

Get your menus right and the rest will follow.

If you have a little time on your hands and yet need some extra money, then this is one of the easiest and quickest ways to get you out of that economic slump.

I know, I've done it and have seen the results for myself.

If you are someone who is prepared to learn and take on board everything you read in this book, set yourself a few targets and aren't frightened of a little hard work, the end result will be a sound profitable business.

And, don't forget, a sound profitable business is an asset that can be sold sometime in the future for a nice profit.

A sandwich business comes in two different varieties, there is the business where you make and deliver sandwiches 'door to door' on a daily basis.

The other sort, which some go straight into while others graduate up to - or do both, is where you prepare sandwiches 'made to order' for business meetings and buffet lunches and maybe even events and functions such as birthday parties, christenings and retirement dos.

Each of these two different sandwich businesses can be made to be very profitable and shows just how much scope there is to be had by simply making and delivering sandwiches.

I will look at these two different sandwich businesses separately, but first I will go through what you will need to get started regardless of which sandwich business you intend to operate.

So, consider everything you are taught in this book and begin to look at the different locations around you. Remember though, with a good sandwich deliver business there are always plenty of opportunities out there if you just keep your eyes open and look.

Also have fun developing your business by putting your stamp and personality on it, but most of all by making that much needed extra cash.

Part One

GETTING STARTED

RESEARCH YOUR AREA

No matter what sort of sandwich delivery business you intend to set up, the first thing you need to do is research your area.

To begin with, one of the first things I found useful was to check out what sort of competition there was in my local area. This is easy enough to do by simply looking through the Yellow Pages and local newspapers.

Don't be too concerned if you find others already doing a sandwich delivery business, as competition is actually good! It means there is a demand.

If you can't find anyone else carrying out this sort of business, don't worry, it just means you need to check a little further to confirm whether or not there is a demand in your area.

Although to be honest, I would be amazed if there wasn't.

The way to do this is to go through the Yellow Pages again and simply phone a few offices or small factory sites and tell them you are considering starting up a sandwich delivery business, and ask if they would be interested in this sort of service.

Bear in mind though that some will say no. But, the secret to setting up a successful sandwich delivery business, as with any other business for that matter, is to carry on and not give up.

Once you have contacted a few different outlets, and got the right feedback from them, you can then go onto the next stage of developing your business.

Begin by making a list of all the different establishments that have shown an interest in your service, or that you think would be interested.

It might even be worth taking a drive around to see what different work places there are in your area.

The sort of places you are looking for are:

Offices – bear in mind that a big office block might have lots of different small companies based in it, and so potentially many different customers.

Even small offices sometimes have a reasonable number of people working there that can't always get out for lunch.

Small factory units – the sort that aren't big enough to have their own canteen or restaurant. If there are any industrial estates, or even retail parks, near you these can make excellent places to call on with sandwiches as often there is nowhere for the employees to get anything to eat.

Small shops – the sort that sell sweets, drinks and high turnover goods are often more than happy to take a batch of sandwiches to sell on a sale or return basis. When I did this I offered the shop owner a 20% commission, which they were more than happy with.

It simply means they have something else to offer their customers without the hassle of having to make it themselves.

Independent supermarkets – if you have any small independent supermarkets in your area these can make extremely good establishments to leave sandwiches with for all the same reasons as above.

So by this stage you have done your research and found that there is a demand for a sandwich delivery business in your area and there is enough establishments to make it viable.

The next step is to sort out what licenses and permits you will need.

LICENSES AND PERMITS

These will obviously depend on what part of the world you want to trade in. As my experience has been with trading in the UK market I am going to deal with this first and then give some information about trading in the US too.

Obviously, whichever side of the 'pond' you live on, the main thing to consider when dealing with food is hygiene. You have to make sure all your work areas are kept scrupulously clean.

I always made sure whenever I was making my sandwiches that I wore latex/plastic gloves and if I was handling raw meat I would remember to change them before handling anything else.

Starting a sandwich business in the UK:

Starting a home based sandwich delivery business in the UK is a reasonably simple process.

Licences And Permits

The first thing you need to do is to contact your local Environmental Health Service and ask for a copy of their Food and Safety Regulations which you will be required to follow. You will probably find your local branch in the Yellow Pages, but if not you could ask at your local Council Offices to see if they have a copy. The Food Standards Agency has a website full of useful information about this subject.

The two main requirements you will have to meet are obtaining a food hygiene certificate and then arranging a visit to your premises by the Environmental Health Officer to pass them fit. If you contact your local council's Environmental Health team they should be able to provide you with a list of suitable food hygiene courses that you can take to obtain your food hygiene certificate.

Once you have received your certificate you can then contact your local Environmental Health Service to arrange for a visit from an Environmental Health Officer.

To find out more go to www.food.gov.uk/business-industry/caterers/startingup where you will find all the information you need on starting up your own catering company. There are also lots of helpful videos on the website so please do take a look.

I would also suggest you look into taking out a Liability Insurance policy, just in case anyone is unfortunate enough to suffer food poisoning from eating your food. As someone said "Better to be safe then sorry".

You will also need to register yourself with your local tax office as a sole trader or partner depending on your situation. I would advise contacting an accountant about this when the time is right.

Starting a sandwich business in the US:

If you wish to start up a sandwich business in the U.S. you will again be required to contact your Local Health Department to secure a permit for your delivery round to carry out your business.

You will need a Food Safety Certificate which you can obtain by contacting your local American Food Safety Institute by calling (800) 723-3873 or by going to the website www.americanfoodsafety.com

The certificate will cover an introduction to food hazards, bacterias, cleaning and sanitation.

You will also be required to have an Environmental Officer check to make sure that you are equipped to keep and transport your sandwiches in a hygienic and safe environment. Also that your premises are suitably hygienic to carry out the task of making your sandwiches.

One other thing you will need is a Vendor License which can be obtained from either your County Administration Offices or your City Hall. This enables the state to collect taxes from your business and is a necessary permit if you want to carry out a business.

A good accountant can help you with this item.

This may all sound an absolutely terrifying process,

but believe me it really is very simple. A lot of the regulations are purely common sense where food hygiene are concerned.

Although I have concentrated on the British and American markets in this chapter it seems to me that whether you are in Canada, Australia, New Zealand, or anywhere for that matter, the same or similar requirements will be needed.

So contacting your local Health Department would be a good place to start and take it from there.

Now that you have discovered that there is a market for a sandwich delivery business in your area and you have either got the licenses and permits sorted out - or at least got the ball rolling - it is time to go onto the next step and work out what prices you will charge and calculate your profit margin.

Read on to find out how to do this.

CALCULATING YOUR PROFIT MARGIN

The difference between a profitable business and one where you are barely making a living is all down to pricing, so working out the right price for your goods is extremely important to say the least.

It doesn't matter whether you are selling sandwiches, or high-end luxury cars – if you price them too high you will find your customer won't buy them. And, if you price them too low you will not make enough money to make your business profitable.

But if you get your prices right then both you and your customers will be happy.

How do you calculate the correct price?

One of the easiest ways is to simply check out what prices your competitors are charging – if you have any.

The more difficult but better way, is to work out what the costs are to make the sandwiches from scratch.

Calculating Your Profit Margin

This will mean buying some ingredients and making a few different sandwiches to work out the actual cost price.

Let's say you want to calculate the price of a tuna mayonnaise sandwich with sweetcorn. Please bear in mind though that prices go up and down all the time so these figures are only for example and will not necessarily be accurate by the time you read this.

To do this you will need to buy:

1 – 800 g medium slice loaf of bread @ 1.35
1 – 3 x 80 g pack of tuna @ 2.22
1 - 1 kg tub of margarine @ 2.98
1 – 750 ml jar of mayonnaise @ 2.00
1 – 326 g can of sweetcorn @ 0.59

Starting with the bread, divide the amount of slices there are in the loaf by two – don't bother counting the crusts though. This is the amount of sandwiches one loaf of bread will make.

Then, divide the price of the loaf by the amount of sandwiches it will make, to calculate the bread cost of each sandwich.

So let's say, for instance, that an 800 g medium sliced loaf of bread contains 22 slices. So the calculation would be:

22 slices divided by 2 = 11 (number of sandwiches)

then

1.35 (cost of the bread) divided by 11 = 0.12

Next empty the tuna into a bowl and mix with 3 - 4 tablespoons of mayonnaise and half a can of sweetcorn. Make sure that you do not add too much mayo and make it too runny.

Spread the margarine onto some slices of bread and apply the tuna mayo mixture onto as many slices as you can while making sure you give a good portion in each sandwich. I find I can make four good portioned sandwiches from these ingredients.

So now you can calculate what your other costs are. Start by looking at how much of the mayonnaise you used to make the four sandwiches. Lets say it was a third of the jar. You used half the can of sweetcorn and 10% of the tub of margarine.

Next times the cost of the mayo by 33% and jot down that price. Then jot down the prices for half the can of sweetcorn and 10% of the margarine.

Add these figure together and divide by four - the amount of sandwiches it all made - then add that figure to the cost of the bread. So your figures might look something like this:

2 slices of bread = 0.12

Tuna = 2.22

Mayo – 2.00 x 33% = 0.66

Sweetcorn – 0.59 x 50% = 0.30

Margarine – 2.98 x 10% = 0.30

2.22 + 0.66 + 0.30 + 0.30 = 3.48 divided by 4 = 0.87

Bread @ 0.12 + Ingredients @ 0.87 = 0.99 (cost price)

And as for the four sandwiches you have made – eat one to judge for yourself if they are up to scratch, and give the others to your family or friends and ask them for their opinion.

Is there enough filling? Are they tasty? Did they like them? The more information you can gain from this exercise the better. And as for you and your family, well you had just better get used to eating and taste testing a lot of different sandwiches.

So, now you have calculated that the cost price of making one tuna mayo sandwich with sweetcorn equals 0.99.

Now you need to know what price you should sell this sandwich for. The good thing about this sort of business is that it has a reasonably high mark-up. That is to say the difference between what it cost to make and the price you charge for it.

I would suggest you look for a 150% margin. That is to say you take the cost price of your sandwich and times that figure by 150%.

0.99 (cost price) x 150% = **1.49** (the mark-up)

then add the mark-up to the cost of the sandwich to work out the selling price.

0.99 + 1.49 = **2.48** (the selling price)

I would round this up to 2.50 and this is what you would look to price and sell this sandwich for. Although it might appear that you are making a whopping big profit on this sandwich, you have to bear in mind that this price does not include any packaging, transport or any other costs involved in making it other than the ingredients.

Now, you might also remember at the beginning of this chapter I suggested you check out what price your competitors were charging so that you had some sort of benchmark. Now you can see exactly why I said that.

If you find that your competitors are only charging 2.20 for their tuna mayo sandwich with sweetcorn, then how difficult do you think its going to be to sell yours for more.

This is where you need to realise that your pricing methods need to be flexible. But at least you now know how to work out the cost price and the selling price using the mark-up percentage. So you simply amend your mark-up percentage so that your price matches your competitors and then you know what mark-up to use for your other range of sandwiches.

If money is rather tight in the area you are looking to operate in then you might find your margins need to be tightened up a bit too. But on the other hand, if you are looking to operate in a much more affluent area, or say in a city centre, then you might just be able to getaway with increasing your mark-up.

This is where all the research comes into it. It is better to find out this information beforehand rather than after you start your business.

Now lets look at what items you will need to run your sandwich business.

ITEMS YOU WILL NEED

Apart from fresh ingredients, which you will need to buy on a daily basis, you will also certainly need to look at buying or having some or all of the following items:

Packaging material – the sandwiches need to be both protected while you are delivering them, but also look professional too. You can use either clear plastic sandwich cases or good quality waxed paper suitable for food, depending on where you live and what sort of sandwich you will be selling.

You might be able to find both of these items at your local cash and carry or, if not, then you will need to look through the Yellow Pages for any local catering supply companies.

As I was catering for the British market I used the plastic sandwich cases as they looked professional plus people could actually see what they were buying.

But, you may want to be more environmental friendly by using the waxed paper wrapping. Do though, bear in mind that they will not protect the sandwiches so they could end up getting squashed and not looking quite so appetising from the customers point of view.

Transport – either a car or a van. If you are just starting out you will probably make use of the family car, but whatever your chosen form of getting you to your destination the vehicle must have enough room to carry all the necessary stock etc.

Obviously as you start your business you will want to keep the running cost as low as you can but please be aware if you continue to use your own family car for any length of time that it might well be advisable to inform your insurance company of this.

Cooler boxes – these are an absolute must to keep all fresh food products chilled, especially during the summer months. They don't have to be anything elaborate, just the sort you would take with you to the beach although obviously the bigger the better.

It might be a good idea to also invest in some extra freezer packs to go in them too.

Vacuum pumps thermos dispenser – this isn't totally necessary to start with unless you are starting out in the winter months and want to offer hot soup along with the sandwiches.

Although I certainly would recommend buying one at a later stage as hot soup can certainly increase your week's takings.

Items You Will Need

Sticky labels – these can be bought from any stationary supplier, of even on line, and come in sheets that fit your printer. Obviously you have to decide first on whether you are going to use the sandwich cases or waxed paper wrapping first, but either way you will be able to find a label to fit your chosen container.

Pricing gun – the sort were you squeeze the handle and it sticks a price tag onto the packaging. These can be found at most stationary outlets.

Trading licenses/Hygiene certificates – this is covered in more detail in the chapter, Licenses and Permits.

Colour Printer – to be honest most homes that have a computer will also have a colour printer, and you will need it to print out not only your labels but also menus too.

THE NEXT STEP

So, now you have completed researching your area for potential customers, checked out any competition, made sure all the necessary licenses and permits are in place, worked out the cost price of your sandwiches, calculated the right amount of percentage mark-up you are going to apply and purchased the various items you will need to run your business.

Now it is time to sit down and put together a menu list.

There is a huge array of different types of breads that can be bought from plain white, brown, granary, tortilla wraps to baguettes, baps, pittas, ciabatas, plus many others too.

All are great tasting, but if you are just starting out I suggest using just three different types of bread, white, brown and maybe a wrap as this keeps it easy and the cost down. I would also recommend that when you buy the loaves of bread you buy the medium sliced loaf as that looks and feels like real value for money.

At the end of the day there is no particular sandwich filling I can advise that will sell the most, because that will depend on your customer's taste. So all you can do is offer a variety to please as many people as possible. I have given you a few ideas for sandwich filling that sold well for me under Recipes.

Once you have made your list, type it up on your computer and print it out making sure it has your contact details on it, and remember to also create a name for your sandwich business too. Keep it straightforward and memorable if you can.

Once you have your menus printed it is time to get your business noticed and the best way to do this is to go and hand deliver your menus to the various businesses you think are potential customers. And don't forget to let them know when you will be starting, by putting the start date on the menu you are handing out.

Depending how your money is situated you may even consider having your own personalised company t-shirt and business cards printed.

But bear in mind the best way of promoting your business and advertising what your business can do is simply word of mouth. And to do that all you have to do is offer a good reliable service at a reasonable price and your customers will recommend your business. Word will soon spread.

ONCE YOU ARE UP AND RUNNING

Once you have your business up and running there are a few other things or services that you will, or may, want to consider buying.

Accountant – some might say you need an accountant right from the very start. All I can say is I didn't contact an accountant until I had the business up and running for a month or two and knew where I was heading.

From what I can see there is a good side and a bad side to using an accountant.

The bad side is that he's there to tell you how much tax you need to pay. Yes even a small business like yours needs to pay tax, especially if you have been dropping off menus to different companies in your area. Take it as read, the tax man will eventually get to hear about you so it is much better to let him know what you are doing before he comes asking. Your accountant will fill out all the relevant paperwork needed for that.

The good side is that you can claim against everything you purchase to carry out and run your business. From the bread and sandwich fillings, the packaging, your vehicles running costs and even the use of your kitchen where you make your sandwiches.

And obviously if you are buying some produce to make sandwiches with but also use some to make a family meal with, you can claim for that too. But if anyone asks I never told you that!

A good accountant can be a god-send, so don't be put off by the idea of contacting one.

How do you find a good accountant? Ask around. Why not ask some of the businesses you deliver to if they could recommend one.

Vehicle signage – at some point you might want to look at having a sign for your vehicle as this is a fantastic way of letting potential customers know who you are and what you do.

I'm not talking about a full vehicle wrap here, just a simple magnetic sign that can be fixed to the door of your car as you carry out your delivery round and then taken off again when not needed.

Wholesale account – once you have been trading a while it might be a good idea to see if you can set up a monthly trading account with your local wholesaler. Any little bit of money you can save means more profit and more money in your pocket, so it really is worthwhile looking into this.

Chest-freezer – I have to say I found a chest-freezer was a really good buy. Trust me, it actually allowed me to buy certain items in bulk which meant I didn't have to go shopping for stock at the end of each day.

Even if you don't want to go for a monthly trading account the chest-freezer will allow you the opportunity to buy loafs of bread and meat items in larger quantities and store them until they are needed.

One word or warning though, please don't do what I did and buy the biggest one I could find thinking I was being clever. I never totally filled it up which meant its running costs were expensive.

This is why I have said to get this once you are up and running because you will know how many loaves of bread and meat you will need for the week. So only buy one that is a little bigger than you actually need which will leave you some extra room as your business grows.

They are not too expensive to buy if you shop around, but remember, it is a business expense and so is tax deductible anyway.

Part Two

OPERATING YOUR BUSINESS

GETTING YOURSELF ORGANISED

The secret to this business is getting yourself organised because there will be a lot to do each morning before you even get out to deliver your sandwiches.

It will also mean an early start in the morning, so I would suggest that you get any meat items that need to be cooked and done the evening before. If you can, once they have cooled down, it would be best to prepare them so they are ready to use the next morning.

This might mean making sure the chicken is diced into chunks, and the bacon cut into pieces and then stored in the fridge overnight. And if you have stored any loaves of bread in the freezer, these will need to be taken out the night before.

This will save you a lot of time the following morning.

Also make sure that any labelling you need for the

packaging is all done and ready to use. That way when the sandwiches are made all you need to do is label them up and you are ready to go.

As I have said before, and I am sure you will have learned this when getting your Food Safety Certificate, it is always best to wear some plastic gloves when making your sandwiches.

When I first started my business I found trying to get everything done in time was quite hectic and stressful, but eventually once I got myself into a routine I found I was much better at using my precious time.

I will now tell you what routine I used.

The first thing I would do was to make sure all the ingredients I needed were prepared and ready to use. This would mean I had all my tomatoes washed and sliced and put into a container ready to use.

The lettuce leaves would be cut, washed and put into a spinner to dry. Any cheese I would be using needed to be grated and put into a container ready to use.

Plus of course all the bread had to be buttered.

So, as you can see there is an awful lot of items that need to have been prepared and ready for you to be able to put the sandwiches together. Now you can see why I said get anything that needs cooking done the night before if you can. The last thing you want to do on a busy morning is to be cooking chicken or bacon and waiting for them to cool down before you can use them.

I would start by choosing a particular filling and begin putting the sandwiches together. I would place the buttered bread onto my work surface and spread the filling onto one piece of bread making sure I went right up to edge with the filling. Then I would top this off with another slice of bread and cut them diagonally across to form a triangle. These two triangles would be placed together and placed into the clear plastic sandwich cases.

If I had started with a cheese filling then I would complete all the different variations of cheese sandwiches, for instance cheese and tomato, cheese and pickle, cheese and onion and cheese ploughman.

Then it is a simple case of doing the same with the other fillings such as the chicken and tuna. I found concentrating on one filling at a time and doing all the different varieties of that filling saved me a lot of time.

This might seem fairly obvious, but believe me it took a few weeks of disorganisation before this hit home.

It doesn't matter whether you are selling your sandwiches door to door or made to order, the initial stages of preparation and putting the sandwiches together will be more or less the same.

Now I want to look at the two different ways of operating a sandwich business along with their pros and cons.

DOOR TO DOOR BUSINESS

As I have said before, everybody needs to eat and you are there to fill that need. Come rain or shine people will come to rely on you to turn up at a regular time and have a variety of different sandwiches available for them to buy.

That will almost certainly mean an early start to your day, and as I described earlier it can also mean quite a hectic one too.

Having completed making all the sandwiches, done all the labelling and packed everything into cooler boxes, you are now ready to hit the road and take in some hard cash. Because at the end of the day that is what it is all about – making money.

Ideally the round you will have researched and found viable will not be too long a drive to get to as time, and hungry customers, wait for no man.

Now it is time to simply stop off at your first call and find out what their lunchtime requirements are. If you are calling at an industrial unit, it could simply be a case of turning up, letting them know you are there and waiting as they come out to your vehicle to chose what they want from the cooler boxes.

In other places, such as offices, it might mean you have to actually go into the building from office to office and take down the orders and fetch them back from your vehicle for them. If that is the case, and it will probably be a mixture of both, it is best to get a little booklet so you can jot down who wants what otherwise you are going to get into a real muddle.

How to increase you daily / weekly sales

I found I could increase my days taking quite substantially by simply offering other items to eat as add-ons. Things like packets of crisps (potato chips), bars of sweets (candy) and of course cans of drink. There is a good profit margin to be made on these sort of items as it is, but because you are bring them to your customers door you can legitimately charge a premium rate for this.

And during the winter months when the weather is really cold you can do even better by offering cups of hot soup. There were days when I would often sell out soup it was so popular. All I did was buy some polystyrene cups and lids and fill up the cups with soup from a vacuum pump thermos dispenser. I have given you a couple of recipes for soup later on in the book.

During the summer months I would offer a salad box which sold really well too. Not only is it lighter for the hot summer months but it is healthy too.

After a while I introduced the idea of offering a 'Friday Special' that became extremely successful. Basically all I did was offer a few sandwich ideas that were a little bit more selective such as Roast Beef and Horseradish, Roast Pork and Stuffing or Prawn Salad. I made sure these were made to look a little more special by serving them in nice wholemeal rolls.

And the best part of all was the fact that I could charge extra for them simply because I marketed them as being a special. You need to make sure you make people aware of this service earlier in the week and take orders on the Thursday so you can buy the ingredients and have it ready for a Friday delivery.

Obviously you are never going to know for certain how many sandwiches you are going to sell from one day to the next so there will be times when you have some sandwiches left over.

What do you do with them? You and your family will eat them of course. Don't forget you are out to earn some extra money, so if you eat these yourself then you won't need to buy anything for your own lunch and so save money.

Supplying shops and small supermarkets

If you have managed to find some small independent supermarkets or shops that will take your sandwiches then this is how I went about it.

I would only call on these sort of establishments three days a week – Monday, Wednesday, and Friday. I would leave a variety of different sandwiches on the Monday stamped with an 'Eat By' date of three days, in other words the Wednesday. I would then take a note in a book of what I had left and the date.

Then on the Wednesday I would call again with a fresh assortment of sandwiches all dated for three days time. If there were any sandwiches left over from what I left on the Monday I would take them away and note what I took in my book.

Then on the Friday I would do the same again, taking away any sandwiches that had not been sold from the Wednesday delivery. And then, as I am sure you have already worked out, I did the same again on the Monday.

Now I had a note of a full weeks supply and return of sandwiches. Some of the owners of these stores were happy to pay on a week by week basis, while others only wanted to pay at the end of each month.

But either way to create there bill I simply added up all the sandwiches I had left on the various days and then subtracted all the sandwiches that had been returned which left me the figure to charge.

When I set this sort of supply and return business up with the owners I offered them a 20% commission, so all I did was deduct the commission owed to them from the total figure and the rest was owed to me. Simple!

I was fortunate enough to have enough of these little

independent stores in my area that after about eighteen months I just concentrated on delivering to them and so only worked three days a week.

As with anything in life there is both good and bad to the door to door sandwich business so lets take a look at what they are.

Pros:

Easy enough to run this business on your own

Cash business

High profit margin

Able to visit multiple sites in one day

Easy to offer add-ons such as crisps, sweets and drinks

Work from home

Only work half day – back home for when the kids finish school

Easy to start-up

Little capital needed

Cons:

Not easy to take time off or fall ill

People may not buy as often when money is tight

Never know how many sandwiches you will sell

Need reliable transport

MADE TO ORDER BUSINESS

The sandwich made to order business is something that you can either graduate up to or start up from scratch. It is more or less the same business from the start-up point of view but rather than preparing sandwiches to go out each day and sell on an ad-hock basis, you only make sandwiches that have been pre-ordered.

Although you would research your business as outlined in this book, you would be more interested in offices and industrial units with the aim of offering to cover their catering needs for meetings and the like.

The days of department heads going out for business lunches that lasted a couple of hours are getting less and less as money is getting tighter. And this makes it an ideal opportunity for you to offer your service providing the food for an in-house meeting.

You can create a set menu to cover various price ranges

or produce a menu on a price per head basis. Really the sky is the limit for this sort of business.

Presentation of not just you but your food is a major part of this business so your packaging requirements would be slightly different.

Instead of plastic sandwich cases you would be better off buying large plastic serving plates where you can arrange an assortment of different sandwiches and then simply cover with cling film.

Obviously you will not just be supplying sandwiches but also finger foods and canapés, some of which you will be able buy ready prepared and others you will have to make yourself.

This sort of business is perhaps more suited to someone with sales person type skills who can negotiate with customers at all different levels, because one day it might be the owner of a small firm and the next day the head of Human Resources for a large corporation organising a big retirement do. Either way you have to be able to not only make the sale – then supply the food to satisfy the customer.

You will be out attending appointments with prospective clients as much, if not more, than actually in your kitchen preparing the food. This is something you have to bear in mind, and it might well be that this sort of business suites more of a partnership rather than just you working on your own.

It might be that your client just wants you to supply the food and leave it to them or it might be that they want you to stay and serve. You need to enquire about this and price it accordingly.

This sort of business, as opposed to the door to door business, which you can get up and running in next to no time, can be much more of a slow burn. You have to face the facts that there may be some weeks where you have one, or even two customers and then other weeks where you don't have any.

That being the case it would be a good idea to place a regular advert in you local paper or even the Yellow Pages. Either a classified or run of print (ROP) ad, whatever you can afford.

Other clients to serve

Although it can be a little slower to get off the ground the scope for this sort of business is huge and it will only be your lack of imagination that holds you back.

Weddings, christenings, funerals, birthday parties – the list just goes on and on, all have the need for your services as well as the locations we have already spoken about.

Many people have started off with this sort of business and then built it up into a full blown outside catering business serving hot foods and employing staff.

If you think that you would like to eventually be running a catering business full time then this business model might be the thing you are looking for.

Let's look at a few of the pros and cons to help you decide.

Pros:

Only making what is needed so little or no waste

Less fuel and time used in making delivery

Could get regular work with big organisations

Easier to take the odd day off if needed

Cons:

You may well be preparing and delivering sandwiches in the mornings and seeing prospective clients in the afternoons

Pressured to meet clients time limit

Presentation must be first class

Would probably need two people to run this business

KEEPING THE BOOKS

Whether you decide to operate a door to door or made to order sandwich business the bookkeeping is pretty straightforward.

With the door to door business I would suggest you take an exercise book with you each day to jot down how many sandwiches you sold and what price they sold for, pretty much as described when supplying shops and supermarkets.

Then either each day, or each week, transfer that information onto a spreadsheet on your computer using Microsoft Excel, or a good alternative is OpenOffice, and what's more it is free too.

Set this up so that it give you a total for the end of each day and then a grand total for the week and month.

This will be as difficult as you make it depending on how much detail you want to see. With my business

I only had three prices for the sandwiches, meat, non-meat and the Friday Special, to make it easy for me.

I also entered onto the spreadsheet any soups and salads I sold plus of course the crisps, sweets and drinks.

On another page on the spreadsheet you will enter all the costs that have been incurred in running your business. This will include any ingredients, packaging, vehicle running costs and sundry items. For sundry items I would list things like labels, ink and such like.

Set this page up so that it shows the amount you spent before any sales tax, the cost of the sales tax and the total including tax. You might only need to do this once you are VAT registered (for the UK), but other countries might want it anyway. Then have the spreadsheet total up all your running costs for the whole month.

You now have all the details to print off and give to your accountant showing how much you have taken, how much you have spent and how much profit you have made.

With that in mind, always make sure you ask for a receipt for anything you buy for the business so you can give these to your accountant too.

If you operate a made to order sandwich business then once again you can more or less follow the simple instructions above.

It is basically about keeping a record of everything that you have taken and everything that you have spent to earn those takings with the receipts to prove it.

RECIPES

At the end of the day there is no sandwich that is guaranteed to sell more than any other, life would be a lot easier if that was the case, it will depend on what your customers want and their tastes will obviously vary.

Some will want a vegetarian sandwich while other will only want a meat sandwich. Your job is to cater for all their tastes and this is something you will learn over time.

I can only tell you here what I found my customers liked – and these are pretty general all-rounders, but only you will know what your customers want in your part of the world.

For me, I found the chicken salad sold really well, along with the cheese ploughman and the tuna mayonnaise on brown was another really good seller.

But as I've already said it all really depends on the customer at the time you call. I've known some customers who had a chicken salad from me day after day for months suddenly decide they wanted a cheese and onion.

You just never can tell, people change their minds just like we do, that is why you need to carry a selection of different fillings.

Over the next couple of pages are some of the recipes that I have used in my sandwich business. I've also included some recipes for soups I made and a couple of cake recipes too.

I don't know you but I love messing around in my kitchen making cakes, whether it be for customers or family, I get a real kick out of it and with my trusty old Kenwood mixer life is so easy whipping up a Victoria Sponge cake with vanilla butter cream or Cinnamon Raisin Swirls.

BLT

Bacon, Lettuce and Tomato

Serves 4

Ingredients

8 - 10 slices of bacon – your choice but I use streaky

1 iceberg lettuce

4 red tomatoes

Mayonnaise

Preparation

Grill the bacon until crispy and put to one side to cool.

Shred the lettuce and slice the tomatoes.

Using a pair of kitchen scissors cut the bacon in to small chunks. Place lettuce, tomato and bacon on bread that has been spread with mayonnaise. If you do it this way round the tomato won't make the bread soggy.

CHICKEN AND SWEETCORN

Serves 4

Ingredients

2 Chicken breasts cooked and diced

160 g cooked sweetcorn

3 - 4 tbsp Mayonnaise

Preparation

Grill the chicken breasts fillets, making sure not to

overcook them, and boil the sweetcorn, allowing both to cool over time.

Once the chicken has cooled cut into small diced chunks, then add the chicken and sweetcorn to a bowl and mix in mayonnaise.

Apply to bread of your choice.

CORONATION CHICKEN
Serves 8

Ingredients

4 skinless, boneless chicken breasts – cooked and diced

1/8 tsp ground black pepper

½ tsp curry powder

175 g (6 oz) mayonnaise

Added options

50 g (2 oz) sultanas

50 g (2 oz) chopped toasted pecans

½ onion chopped

Lettuce leaves

Preparation

I find it best to buy the chicken breasts that have been filleted as they are nice and thin and cook quicker. Cook these for about 5 minutes each side or until they are cooked through then put them to one side to cool down.

Once cooled cut into small diced chunks. Combine chicken, curry powder, mayonnaise, pepper and any of the added options into a bowl.

Mix together until the mixture resembles a pale yellow colour. Ensuring all the chicken is evenly coated.

Spread evenly over bread of your choice and add a few slices of lettuce leaves.

Note: To reduce fat and calories use only half the mayonnaise and add the other half as créme fraiche.

CHICKEN SALAD

Serves 4

Ingredients

2 chicken breasts – cooked & diced

1 pack cherry tomatoes

6 tbsp mayonnaise

Optional ingredients

Grapes sliced into quarters

Celery

Preparation

Grill the chicken breasts until cooked through and put to one side to cool down. Place the cooked, diced chicken in a bowl and combine tomatoes, and mayo along with grapes and celery if wanted.

Allow to chill for a 5 – 10 minutes. Serve on bread of your choice along with lettuce leaves and tomatoes.

ALL DAY BREAKFAST

Serves 6

Ingredients

1 Packet Bacon, cooked

1 Packet Cumberland sausages, cooked

4 Hard Boiled Eggs

4 tbsp Mayonnaise

Preparation

Cook bacon and sausages and leave to cool.

Place the eggs in cold water and bring to boil, turn off the heat and leave for a further 10 minutes.

Peel eggs and mash together with the mayonnaise.

When bacon has cooled use kitchen scissors to cut into small pieces.

Once sausages are cold slice in half and together with the bacon, eggs and mayonnaise mix add to your bread.

You can use this recipe to make a similar sandwich for Bacon and Egg.

BACON AND EGG

Serves 4

Ingredients

8 eggs hard boiled

8 - 10 slices of bacon – your choice but I use streaky

8 tbsp mayonnaise

Salt and pepper to season

Optional ingredients

1 tsp mustard

¼ tsp paprika

Preparation

Place eggs in a saucepan of boiling water with a little salt added to it for about 3 – 4 minutes. Turn off the heat and leave to stand in the water for a further 10 minutes.

Take the eggs out of the water and leave to one side to cool, once cool to the touch peel off the shell. Place the peeled eggs into a large bowl along with the mayo, mustard and paprika (if you so wish).

Grill the bacon until crispy and leave to cool.

Using the back of a fork mash the eggs and mayo together and season with salt and pepper.

Using a pair of kitchen scissors cut the bacon in to small chunks and add to the mixture of egg mayonnaise.

Now add to your bread and hey presto you have a tasty lunchtime sandwich.

TUNA SALAD
Serves 6

Ingredients

1 tin (400 g) tuna in brine, drained

2 sticks of celery finely chopped

6 tbsp mayonnaise

2 tbsp finely chopped gherkin (dill pickle) - *optional*

Salt and pepper to taste

Optional ingredients

2 tbsp finely chopped onion

Preparation

Mix all ingredients in a bowl and stir thoroughly making sure the tuna has a good coating of mayonnaise. Add the salt and pepper to taste.

Spread evenly over bread of your choice and add slices of lettuce and tomatoes.

TUNA MAYO WITH SWEETCORN
Serves 4

Ingredients

240 g tuna in brine

160 g cooked sweetcorn

3 - 4 tbsp mayonnaise

Preparation

Drain the tuna and dry off using kitchen roll. Empty

into a bowl along with the cooked sweetcorn and mayonnaise.

Mix together well. Add the mixture to bread of your choice.

EGG MAYO

Serves 4

Ingredients

8 eggs
8 tbsp mayonnaise
1 tsp Dijon mustard – optional
1/4 tsp paprika
Salt and pepper to taste

Preparation

Place eggs in boiling water with a little salt added to it for about 3 – 4 minutes. Turn off the heat and leave to stand in the water for a further 10 minutes.

Take the eggs out of the water and leave to one side to cool, once cool to the touch peel off the shell. Place the peeled eggs into a large bowl along with the mayo, mustard (if you so wish) and season with the paprika and salt and pepper.

Using the back of a fork mash them all together and spread onto buttered bread.

This tastes great on granary or white bread and even in a tortilla.

CHEESE PLOUGHMAN

Serves 4

Ingredients

200 g strong cheddar cheese – or similar

225 g cherry tomatoes

iceberg lettuce

4 tbsp spreadable pickle

Preparation

Grate the cheddar cheese into a bowl.

Wash and then cut the cherry tomatoes into quarters.

Wash and tear the lettuce leaves.

Butter your bread, granary is really nice with this as it adds a rustic touch to the meal.

Spread the lettuce, cherry tomatoes and grated cheddar to one half and spread the pickle to the other half of the sandwich.

This recipe can be used with chicken or even ham.

TOMATO SOUP

Serves 8 - 10

Ingredients

400 ml tomato sauce - concentrated

2 litres milk - full fat

Oregano

Salt and pepper

Preparation

This recipe is not only delicious but is extremely easy too. Simply empty the tomato sauce into a large bowl and stir in the milk. Sprinkle on some dried oregano for more flavour.

Gradually warm the soup remembering to stir continually. Do not let it come to the boil but make sure it is heated through. Add salt and pepper to taste and then pour into a vacuum pump thermos dispenser to keep warm as you go about your delivery round.

These soup recipes are a real money maker during the winter months, but are also fantastic to have at home too.

CARROT AND CORIANDER SOUP

Serves 6

Ingredients

900 g carrots, peeled and chopped

1 tbsp coriander seeds

25 g butter

1 small garlic clove, crushed

Vegetable stock cube

Salt and pepper

Preparation

Over a medium heat, dry roast the coriander seeds for about two minutes until they look toasted. Then grind them in a pestle and mortar until they are course.

Heat the butter in a large pan and add the chopped carrots, garlic and three-quarters of the coriander seeds. Cover the pad and leave over a gentle heat for about ten minutes.

Mix the stock cube in 1.2 litres of boiling water and add to the pan. Bring to the boil then simmer for 15 – 20 minutes with the pan partially covered until the vegetables are soft.

Using a blender puree the soup down until it is completely smooth. Add salt and pepper to taste.

BUTTERNUT SQUASH SOUP

Serves 6 – 8

Ingredients

2 kg butternut squash

1 medium sized red pepper

30 g butter

1 tbsp olive oil

2 onions, peeled and chopped

2 tbsp thyme

2 vegetable stock cubes

Salt and pepper

Preparation

Turn your oven up to 190º C / gas mark 5, while that is warming up scoop the seeds from the butternut squash and cut the red pepper in half.

Put them onto a baking tray and place them into the hot oven for about an hour or until they are both cooked through and tender.

Using a large pan heat the oil and butter then add the onion and, over a medium heat, cook for around 5 – 8 minutes or until the onion has softened. Stir occasionally to make sure it does not burn.

When the butternut squash and red pepper have cooked remove the skin from the butternut squash and place the flesh in the pan with the onions. Cut the pepper into small chunks and add them into the pan too. Add the thyme also.

Crumble the stock cube into 1 litre of boiling water and stir till the stock cube has dissolved. Add this to the pan and bring to the boil then simmer for 20 minutes.

Remove from the heat and using a blender puree until it is all smooth and season to taste.

VICTORIA SPONGE CAKE

Serves 6-8

Ingredients

3 Medium Eggs

175 g butter, softened

175 g caster sugar

175 g Self Raising Flour

Set oven at Gas Mark 5 or 190 C.

Preparation

Add softened butter and caster sugar to bowl and cream together. Slowly combine eggs into the mixture, I normally begin to add flour as well as I don't want everything to curdled.

Now beat the mixture until light and fluffy.

Divide the cake mix between two greased sandwich tins and bake in center of the oven for 20 - 25 minutes or until the cake has risen.

A good way to test the cake is baked through is to push the centre of the cake and see if it springs back into shape.

Remove cake from the oven and leave to cool for 5-10 minutes before turning out on to a wire rack.

While the cake is cooling down I use this time to make the butter cream for the centre.

Please see butter cream recipe on the next page.

VANILLA BUTTER CREAM

Ingredients

260 g icing sugar

2 tbsp softened unsalted butter

2 tbsp milk

1 tsp vanilla essence

Preparation

Place the butter in a bowl and cream, slowly adding the sifted icing sugar, milk and vanilla essence.

When all the ingredients have been added you should have a mixture that is firm but easy to apply to the cake.

If the mixture is too running you will need to add more icing sugar.

I tend to do a Victoria Sponge Cake with both vanilla butter cream and strawberry jam.

This sells well and if there is any left over it doesn't last long in my house.

CINNAMON RAISIN SWIRLS

Serves 16

This is such and easy recipe and one I cheat with but shhhh I won't tell if you don't.

Ingredients

1 packet of ready made Puff Pasty (no one will ever

know you've not made it yourself)

75 g unsalted butter

75 g caster sugar

2 tsp cinnamon spice

60 g raisins

One egg mixed with milk for glaze.

Preparation

Heat oven to 200° C/fan180° C/gas 6. While oven is heating up, roll out your pasty to approximately 30cm x 40cm rectangle on a floured board.

Some recipes will tell you to beat the butter, sugar and cinnamon together. That is okay if you have time, but for me I place all 3 ingredients into a saucepan and gently heat until butter is melted and all ingredients are absorbed.

Place your melted mixture over the pasty and scatter raisins on top. Now roll the pasty to make a sausage shape and place in the refrigerator and chill for 10 minutes. Then with a serrated knife divide into 16 slices.

Lay the slices flat onto a baking tray, cut side down, and brush with the egg glaze. Bake for 18 - 20 minutes or until golden brown.

These are delicious and sell really quickly.

METRIC CONVERSIONS

Here is a simple guide for converting metric measurements into American equivalent that might be of some help to you.

Liquids

5 ml = 1 teaspoon
15 ml = 1 tablespoon or 1/2 fluid ounce
30 ml = 1 fluid ounce or 1/8 cup
60 ml = 1/4 cup or 2 fluid ounces
80 ml = 1/3 cup
120 ml = 1/2 cup or 4 fluid ounces
160 ml = 2/3 cup
180 ml = 3/4 cup or 6 fluid ounces
240 ml = 1 cup or 8 fluid ounces or half a pint
350 ml = 1 1/2 cups or 12 fluid ounces
475 ml = 2 cups or 1 pint or 16 fluid ounces
700 ml = 3 cups or 1 1/2 pints
950 ml = 4 cups or 2 pints or 1 quart
3.8 litre = 4 quarts or 1 gallon

Weight

28 g = 1 ounce
113 g = 4 ounces or 1/4 pound
150 g = 1/3 pound
230 g = 8 ounces or 1/2 pound
300 g = 2/3 pound
340 g = 12 ounces or 3/4 pound

450 g = 1 pound or 16 ounces
900 g = 2 pounds

Non liquid ingredients

110 g Flour, well sifted all purpose (wheat) = 1 cup
200 g Sugar, granulated cane = 1 cup

Temperature

100º C = 212 ºF

IN CONCLUSION

No matter whether you are looking to make a little extra income, or even a full-time living, I am sure you will now recognise what an opportunity a sandwich delivery business is.

Whether you decide to operate a door to door, or made to order business I am sure you can see what huge potential either of these businesses can offer you.

I have used the knowledge and experience gained from my own business to show you how to set up and run your own profitable sandwich business from scratch.

I hope you have enjoyed reading this book and found the information helpful, if that is the case I would appreciate it if you would post a positive review of this book.

Many thanks
Jane Thomas

HISTORY OF THE HUMBLE SANDWICH

It is said that Hillel the Elder, a Jewish sage wrapped meat in a soft Matzah, a flat, unleavened bread during the Jewish festival of Passover, thus producing today's sandwich wrap.

In the Middle Ages, slabs of stale bread were used as plates, "trenchers". Once the meal was over these trenchers were given to feed either the dog or local beggars.

The trenchers, technically became today's open sandwich.

The sandwich became popular in Spain and England during the rise of the industrial revolution, to the working classes the sandwich was easy to make, portable and inexpensive.

During the 19th Century the sandwich started to

appear outside Europe, and by the early 20th century bread had become the staple diet of most American families.

Around this time the sandwich became a popular lunchtime food.

The name sandwich was the namesake of John Montague, 4th Earl of Sandwich, from the village of Sandwich which nestles in the beautiful county of Kent, in The Garden of England.

OTHER BOOKS BY THIS PUBLISHER

Cayenne Pepper Health Benefits

 I have written this book as a follow on from my other two successful books on Cayenne Pepper - Cure Sore Throats, Colds and Coughs with Cayenne Pepper and How to Lower High Blood Pressure using Cayenne Pepper. I decided to write this book because I realised so many people were looking for a more natural way to treat their health problems.

That is why I have tried to show you all the different benefits that can be found in cayenne pepper. Or as Dr. Richard Schulze, the famed medical herbalist put it, -

"If you master only one herb in your life, master cayenne pepper. It is more powerful than any other."

In this book you will learn how cayenne pepper can help heal such ailments as -

Blood Pressure, Arthritis, Allergies, Sinusitis, Tooth Ache . . . and even Cancer

I have included recipes for the different doses and mixtures and have even included a chapter on making your own cayenne infused oil and cayenne tincture.

How to Lower Hight Blood Pressure using Cayenne Pepper

Be sure to read this book if you want to learn how to cure "the silent killer." It is estimated that around one third of all adults suffer from high blood pressure.

Even more concerning is the fact that a great deal of them are unaware they even suffer from the condition.

More people suffer from high blood pressure now than at any other time!

This book gives vital information on how to lower and even cure high blood pressure.

In this book you will learn:

What the effects of high blood pressure are

How cayenne pepper is a natural cure for high blood pressure

How to use cayenne to lower high blood pressure

And, how to prevent high blood pressure in the first place

This is a GREAT little guide book for learning How to Lower High Blood Pressure Using Cayenne Pepper that I am sure you will benefit from.

Cure Sore Throats, Colds and Coughs with Cayenne Pepper

Once the sore throat and aching limbs of a cold begin, what you need is something that will quickly relieve the symptoms and get you back onto the road to recovery. Cayenne pepper is the very thing.

Although there are many over the counter products that claim to be able to do this, cayenne pepper is a natural product that has a huge healing benefit.

Learn how using this secret miracle cure will relieve the symptoms of a cold quickly and easily.

Miracle is not a work used lightly to describe the healing benefits of Cayenne Pepper.

This book describes in detail the usage and directions for each step to cure a sore throat, cold and cough.

For anyone wanting a more natural approach to recover from a cold or flu like symptoms then Cayenne Pepper should be at the top of your list.

In this book you will learn:

The different recipes and dosages to be taken for each stage of the cold.

The benefits and reasons why they help you . . .

. . . and, how often to use them.

The healing properties of this natural spice should not be taken lightly, its benefits go way beyond just relieving a cold or flu and these benefits are also listed in this book.

Affirmations for Health, Wealth and Happiness

We are all looking for health, wealth and happiness - but few of us ever find it. Probably because we don´t know how to go about finding it.

But this illustrated book of affirmations will teach you how!

I am sure you have all heard of affirmations before, maybe even used one or two over the years, but did you ever realize how important affirmations are and the effect they have on you?

In this book you will learn:

Why affirmations are so important.

What positive affirmations are.

Why you should use them.

How often to use them . . .

. . . and, find examples of affirmations you can use for health, wealth and happiness, plus also affirmations for anxiety, career, love, self-esteem, gratitude and weight loss.

This is a GREAT little guide book of affirmations.

www.ingramcontent.com/pod-product-compliance
Lightning Source LLC
Chambersburg PA
CBHW071619170526
45166CB00003B/1107